Twitter and Tweet

Bringing Home a Bird

by Amanda Doering Tourville

illustrated by Andi Carter

Special thanks to our advisers for their expertise:

Sharon Hurley, D.V.M.
New Ulm (Minnesota) Regional
Veterinary Center

Terry Flaherty, Ph.D., Professor of English
Minnesota State University, Mankato

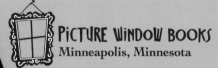

PICTURE WINDOW BOOKS
Minneapolis, Minnesota

Get a Pet

Editor: Jill Kalz
Designer: Hilary Wacholz
Page Production: Michelle Biedscheid
Art Director: Nathan Gassman
Associate Managing Editor: Christianne Jones
The illustrations in this book were created with mixed media.
Photo Credit: Joanne Harris and Daniel Bubnich/
Shutterstock, 23

Picture Window Books
151 Good Counsel Drive
P.O. Box 669
Mankato, MN 56002-0669
877-845-8392
www.picturewindowbooks.com

Printed in the United States of America.

All books published by Picture Window Books
are manufactured with paper containing at least
10 percent post-consumer waste.

Library of Congress Cataloging-in-Publication Data
Tourville, Amanda Doering, 1980-
Twitter and tweet : bringing home a bird / by
Amanda Doering Tourville ; illustrated by Andi Carter.
p. cm. – (Get a pet)
Includes index.
ISBN 978-1-4048-4865-8 (library binding)
1. Cage birds–Juvenile literature. I. Carter, Andi, 1976-, ill.
II. Title.
SF461.35.T68 2008
636.6'8–dc22
2008006452

Table of Contents

A New Bird

Erin is getting a pet bird! Before she goes to the pet store, she reads about all kinds of birds. What kind of bird will she get today? Will she buy a large bird or a small bird? What color will it be?

TIP

Pet stores aren't the only places that have birds. Check the want ads in the newspaper. Stop in at an animal shelter or bird rescue center. Ask a veterinarian for a list of local breeders.

Having a bird is a lot of fun, but it is also a lot of work. Is Erin ready?

Most Popular Bird Breeds
Parakeet (Budgerigar)
Cockatiel
Finch
Canary
Lovebird

Choosing a Bird

With so many kinds of birds, choosing the best one is hard.

Macaw

Parrot

Canary

TIP
No matter what kind of bird you choose, make sure it is healthy. A healthy bird is active. It has bright eyes and smooth feathers.

Cockatiel

Parrots and macaws are large and colorful. But they don't always make the best pets. Parakeets and cockatiels are good pets. They like people. But they need a lot of attention. Other small birds, such as finches and canaries, are easy to keep. But they don't like to be touched.

Erin chooses a parakeet. She names him Roy.

Parakeet

Finch

Canary

Coming Home

Erin's new bird is home! But he is a little scared. Everything is new to him. Erin puts her bird and his cage in a quiet spot. She gives him a few days to get used to the new place.

Birds need a lot of exercise. Erin lets her bird fly around the family room. She watches him carefully so he stays safe. Birds also like to climb. Erin's bird has his own jungle gym.

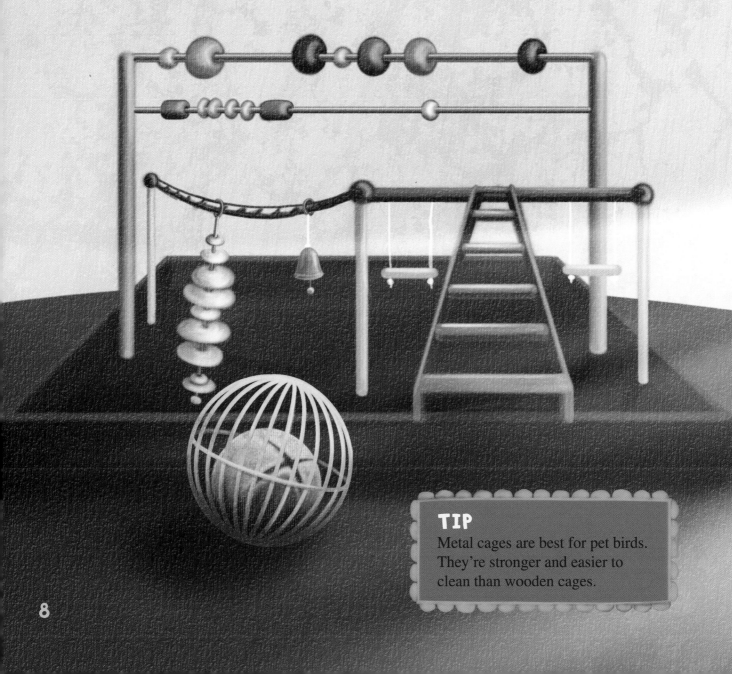

TIP
Metal cages are best for pet birds. They're stronger and easier to clean than wooden cages.

Erin likes toys, and so does her bird! Pet stores sell lots of toys to keep birds busy.

Time to Eat

Erin feeds her bird special bird food she buys at the pet store. She also gives her bird bits of fruit and vegetables. Apples and carrots are his favorites. Erin feeds her bird every day and gives him fresh water twice a day.

Birds need calcium and other minerals that sometimes can't be found in food. Erin gives her bird cuttlebones and mineral blocks to peck at. She buys these things at the pet store, too.

TIP
Never feed your bird chocolate or give him a sip of your soda. These things can make your bird sick and even kill him.

Grooming

Birds love to play in water. While they're playing, they're also getting clean. Erin gives her bird a small tub of room-temperature water to bathe in. She changes the water every day.

Birds groom their own feathers. They puff them out, peck at them, and then smooth them down with their bill.

TIP
Your bird might also need to have his claws clipped. Let your parents or an animal groomer clip your bird's claws.

Keeping Clean

Birds are messy animals. Erin changes the dirty paper or litter at the bottom of her bird's cage every day. She washes and dries his food and water bowls, too.

TIP

Soap and other household cleaners can be harmful to your bird. Pet stores sell pet-safe cleaners that you can use to clean your bird's cage.

Once a week, Erin cleans her bird's cage. First, she puts her bird in a safe place. Then, she cleans the cage with hot, soapy water. She makes sure to rinse it and dry it completely. Erin also washes and dries her bird's toys and perches.

Staying Healthy

Birds need checkups just like people do. Shortly after getting her bird, Erin takes him to the vet. The vet tells Erin her bird is healthy. The vet also answers questions Erin has about her bird.

TIP

Never keep your bird's cage in or near the kitchen. Cooking fumes can make your bird very sick.

Once Erin gets to know her bird, she will know when he isn't feeling well. He may sleep more than usual. He may stop eating. He may stop grooming his feathers. If Erin thinks her bird is sick, she takes him to the vet right away.

Good Night, Bird!

Erin's bird goes to bed when she does, but he wakes up with the sun. That can be very early! Erin puts her bird's cage in an area of the house away from the bedrooms so everyone can sleep. The cage gets plenty of sunlight during the day and is dark at night.

TIP

If you have problems with your bird staying up too late or waking up too early, you can cover his cage with a towel. That way he will be able to sleep as long as you do.

A Happy Pet

Taking care of a bird is a lot of work! But it's also a lot of fun. Erin's bird counts on her to keep him healthy and happy. If Erin takes good care of her bird, she will have a feathered friend for a long time!

Parakeet Close-up

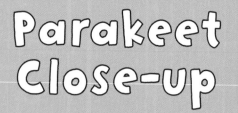

A parakeet breathes and smells through a fleshy bump on its bill called a **CERE**.

A parakeet's **EYES** are on the sides of its head. To see forward, the bird must turn its head.

The bones inside a parakeet's **WING** are hollow and weigh very little.

A parakeet's **BILL** never stops growing. The bird must keep pecking to wear it down.

TAIL FEATHERS help a parakeet steer while in flight.

Parakeet **CLAWS** are made of the same material that human fingernails are.

A parakeet has four **TOES** on each foot— two point forward, and two point backward.

Parakeet Life Cycle

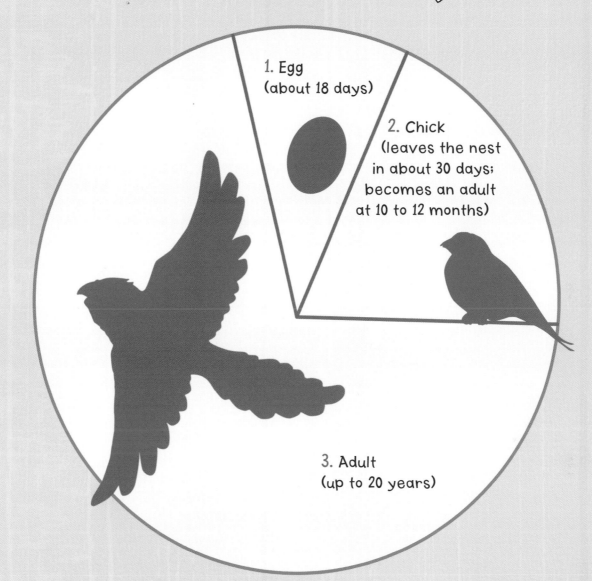

1. Egg
(about 18 days)

2. Chick
(leaves the nest
in about 30 days;
becomes an adult
at 10 to 12 months)

3. Adult
(up to 20 years)

Glossary

animal shelter—a safe place where lost or homeless pets can stay

breed—a kind or type

breeder—a person who raises animals to sell

groom—to clean and make an animal look neat

litter—a material that draws in an animal's waste

perch—a support, such as a stick or peg, on which a bird rests

veterinarian—a doctor who takes care of animals; vet, for short

Parakeet

To Learn More

More Books to Read

Loves, June. *Birds.* Philadelphia: Chelsea Clubhouse, 2004.

MacAulay, Kelley, and Bobbie Kalman. *Parakeets.* New York: Crabtree Pub. Co., 2005.

Preszler, June. *Caring for Your Bird.* Mankato, Minn.: Capstone Press, 2008.

Stewart, Melissa. *Small Birds.* New York: Benchmark Books, 2003.

On the Web

FactHound offers a safe, fun way to find Web sites related to topics in this book. All of the sites on FactHound have been researched by our staff.

1. Visit *www.facthound.com*
2. Type in this special code: 1404848657
3. Click on the FETCH IT button.

Your trusty FactHound will fetch the best sites for you!

Index

Look for all of the books in the Get a Pet series:

Flutter and Float: Bringing Home Goldfish
Purr and Pounce: Bringing Home a Cat
Scurry and Squeak: Bringing Home a Guinea Pig
Skitter and Scoot: Bringing Home a Hamster
Twitter and Tweet: Bringing Home a Bird
Woof and Wag: Bringing Home a Dog